Regards From A Friend

GEORGE LEE

Compiled by David Tadman

UNIQUE PUBLICATIONS, Inc.
4201 Vanowen Place
Burbank, CA 91505
www.cfwenterprises.com

First published in 2002 by
CFW Enterprises, Inc.

ISBN: 0-86568-217-8
Library of Congress Catalog Number: 2002012908
Distributed by:
Unique Publications
4201 Vanowen Place
Burbank, CA 91505
(800) 332-3330

First edition
05 04 03 02 01 00 99 98 97 1 3 5 7 9 10 8 6 4 2

Printed in the United States of America

Editor: Doug Jeffrey
Design: Willy Blumhoff Design

George Lee:
"The Master Maker"

George Lee was more than a good friend of the legendary Bruce Lee; he was a revolutionist in his own right. He spent countless hours that turned into days and sometimes months, creating Bruce's workout equipment.

For George's hard work, dedication and expertise, Bruce called him, "The Master Maker." In addition to this accolade, George should also be known as "The Master of Friendship," because his reliability, dependability and friendship were unparalleled.

Thus, to George Lee, a dedicated friend and a man who always truthfully expresses himself, this book is also for you.

— David Tadman

Editor's Note

With the exception of a few private comments from Bruce Lee, these letters were transcribed just as he wrote them.

Dedication

I would like to dedicate this book to the memory of Bruce Lee, my teacher and friend, and to the spirit of *jeet kune do*.

To be sure, Bruce was a true innovator of life. One does not have to study martial arts to experience the art of Bruce Lee's philosophy. Jeet kune do can be found in the songwriter's songs or the painter's paintings.

Bruce Lee did not believe in styles or doctrines, nor did he believe in set patterns. He believed in self-examination and self-realization, both of which lead to truthfully expressing one's self. The name jeet kune do is only a group of words to remind you that you are in the process of self-exploration.

So, to all the martial artists and painters and songwriters, I also dedicate this book to you.

— George Lee

Acknowledgements

"To share with family and friends is to be fulfilled."

There are several people I would like to thank, starting with my wife, Mary. She has shown me incredible support and love through all the years we have been together.

I would like to thank Linda and Shannon Lee for their inspiration and friendship. My appreciation can't be measured in words. They conquered many obstacles with love, compassion and understanding; they are true heroes.

I would like to thank David Tadman for inspiring me to do this book. David composed this book out of love and the search to know more about a man he calls his hero, Bruce Lee.

I would like to thank Willy Blumhoff for his help and artistry in making this book a graphic treasure. A special thanks goes out to Doug Jeffrey at CFW for his help in this creative process. Thank you also to Jose Fraguas and Michael James at CFW Enterprises.

Finally, I would like to thank all the wonderful family and friends with whom I have had the privilege of sharing precious times.

— George Lee

Contents

BRUCE LEE'S
TAO OF
CHINESE GUNG FU

振 藩 拳 道

以無法爲有法

以無限爲有限

一九六六年十一月廿七日

李振藩

此證

滿准予升入第二級

縣人在館修練期

學生李鴻新係加省

Richmond

Date *Nov. 27 1966*

This is to certify that

George Lee

*Is personally taught by Bruce Lee, and having fulfilled
the necessary requirements, is hereby promoted to* **Second**
rank in Bruce Lee's Tao of Chinese Gung Fu.

BRUCE LEE

Foreword

By George Lee

I met Bruce Lee in the early 1960s. From the time of our first meeting until his passing in 1973, we remained good friends.

To me, Bruce Lee was a very special person on many fronts. He was a revolutionary in the world of martial arts as well as a philosophical prophet. He was also a man with a vision, and he let nothing stand in his way of accomplishing that vision. Bruce was a self-made man, and he made his dreams reality.

I was very fortunate to have known Bruce. I was truly blessed to have shared precious moments with him and to be included in his search of himself, his art and his life.

Bruce Lee can never be compared to any other martial artist or philosopher. He was truly in a league all his own. What made him great was the journey he took of self-discovery and self-determination. Bruce saw his goals and willed those goals. And in the end, he always accomplished what he set out to do.

Bruce was determined to let nothing stand in his way. In fact, I believe he welcomed obstacles. He knew that if he overcame these problems, it would make him stronger and more determined in his path of self-enlightenment.

Bruce's Teaching Philosophy

Years before I met Bruce, I studied kung-fu. When Bruce came into my life and opened my eyes to his way of training, I knew then that all of my previous martial arts training was obsolete. I put all my past training aside and became a disciple, so to speak.

I was some years older than Bruce. Therefore, at first, it was strange that this young man was teaching me. However, it only took a few lessons for me to realize that he was doing something special. Bruce was able to relate to people — regardless of age, race or religion — in a way I have never seen. When you took his class, all of those things did not mean anything. And you, as an individual, were the same as everyone else.

Bruce and I had many lunches and dinners together, and we conversed about a variety of topics, including martial arts and philosophy. Bruce was a truthful and giving man who truly wanted the best for you.

George Lee (right) practicing kung-fu techniques with a friend.

He not only taught you the physical and philosophical side of the martial arts, but he also covered the psychological aspects. He always wanted you to be prepared in every situation. On several occasions, I remember walking into class and — without any warning — he screamed my name. Without giving it a second thought, I would respond with a loud yell, "Yes!" That was simply Bruce's way of keeping you on your toes. He would always do little things like that to keep your awareness up.

It seems now, in retrospect, that Bruce had seemed to conquer the mental, physical, and — almost — the spiritual. I say almost because he was in the process of doing so when unfortunately he passed away. I believe that if one conquers these three levels in life then one will conquer himself.

Bruce's Training Equipment

My friendship with Bruce went beyond the training we

shared. We also collaborated in the construction of many pieces of equipment he used for his personal training. Bruce would come to me with an idea for training equipment, and I would make his vision come to life.

I am truly honored that I was an important friend in Bruce's life and that I had contributed in his expression of his physical being. Bruce and I spent countless times designing equipment and going over diagrams and ideas that gave that equipment life. When they were completed, he used them in his daily training.

When I see Bruce in his films, I feel proud that his physical stature had something to do with the equipment that I made for him. Bruce was truly serious about his physical training. The equipment I made for him helped him in his search for a better, stronger and healthier body. Bruce put his trust in me and felt he could share with me one of the most important things in his life: the development of his physical being. I feel honored that he put that trust in me, and I truly miss those times we spent together, creating the machines that helped him in his search for physical perfection.

The Unforgettable Words

When Bruce was becoming more famous in the world of television and film, we saw less of one another. Despite his hectic schedule, however, he always kept in contact with me via letters.

Throughout the years that Bruce and I shared as friends, he would occasionally send me letters that touched on a variety of topics, including his career, his martial arts and physical development, the machines I built or the equipment he wanted me to build for him. Most of all, these letters show just how much Bruce appreciated me as a friend.

The letters in this book show much more than Bruce Lee the film legend, Bruce Lee the martial arts legend or the philosophical prophet. These unforgettable words show Bruce Lee the human being, the friend and the artist who was in search of self-expression. I held on to the memorable words in these letters for years, occasionally looking at them and remembering the special times they represented.

Nowadays, you can go to a bookstore and find many publications on Bruce Lee, from his martial art training to a memorial tribute. I believe all these books help keep Bruce Lee's legacy alive.

In this book, however, I wanted to show Bruce from a different perspective. Thus, when you read these letters, picture them as personal correspondence from Bruce Lee to you. By doing this, you will get a small glimpse into what I experienced as his student — and most of all — his friend. So read this book not as an outsider, but as someone who shared in the experience.

— George Lee

"To share one's riches is to enrich others."

"Regards from Bruce Lee"

*I*n the early 1960s, George Lee met an amazing man — Bruce Lee. George Lee and Bruce Lee became friends on many different levels. There was the teacher-student relationship, the artist-creator relationship and most of all, there was the close friendship they had until Bruce Lee's passing in 1973. On the following pages, you will experience the closeness these two men shared.

George and Bruce in front of the L.A. Chinatown school.

Regards From A Friend

Letters to George

*I*n his letters, Bruce always used to tell me what was happening in his life. When I look at this letter, I remember great moments of going out to eat with him and discussing the martial arts, as well as how his career was going. Bruce and I shared many moments like this.

Dear George,

I'll be going to New York on the 1st of May then to Wash. D.C. for an appearance. After that I'll go to Seattle for two day and will stop by Oakland for a day before returning home. It will probably be on May 10 that I'll stop by Oakland at that time let's get together and have a Gung Fu session.

The latest is that Greenway Production will most likely pick up my contract ----- a one hr. series is in the planning.

Take Care.

Bruce

Dear George,

I'll be going to New York on the 1st of May then to Wash. D. C. for an appearance. After that, I'll go to Seattle for two days and will stop by Oakland for a day before returning home. It will probably be on May 10 that I'll stop by Oakland. At that time let's get together and have a Gung Fu session.

The latest is that Greenway Production will most likely pick up my contract — a one year series is in the planning.

Take care

Bruce

The students from the Oakland class gather at James Lee's house.

*W*hen I read this letter, it takes me back to the time when Bruce and I hung out together at Wally Jay's luau. Good friends and great conversations always surrounded times like that.

Dear George,

I'm planning to come up for Wally's luau and at the same time to go to Jame's class in Fremont. Understand that class consist mostly Chinese.

I'll fly up on Friday (Nov 3) and James class is that same night so if you have nothing previously planned, it might be beneficial for you to attend that class. I'm going to teach a public class ——— it has been a long time. Say, maybe you can go to the luau tho.

Anyway, I'll talk to you when I'm up there. If you likes to attend the Fremont class for that night, contact James.

Take Care my friend

Best regard to your wife

Bruce Lee

Dear George,

I'm planning to come up for Wally's luau and at the same time to go to James' class in Fremont. Understand that class consists of mostly Chinese.

I'll fly up on Friday (Nov. 3) and James class is that same night. So if you have nothing previously planned, it might be beneficial for you to attend that class. I'm going to teach a public class — it has been a long time. Say, maybe you can go to the luau too.

Anyway, I'll talk to you when I'm up there. If you like to attend the Fremont Class for this night, contact James.

Take care my friend

Best regard to your wife

Bruce Lee

Bruce looking sharp for a school photo.

*B*ruce was excited about the possibility of getting a role on the television show "Hawaii Five-O." Unfortunately, that never materialized.

Dear George,

Your work, everyone of them, is fantastic. Not only are they professional, they are simply artistic. As usual, everyone here has high praise for your art. I, myself, do appreciate very much for your taking time off to do all these wonderful things for me. Thanks a lot George.

I'm sorry to say that I've lost your lists for autograph. So will you please send me another one. Tell Dave Young of the delay too.

Upon my arrival, my agent called to let me know of CBS. proposal for a one hr. serial — kind of like I spy called "Hawaii 50". Looks good. will let you know what develops. (over)

will probably start tour next month but
somehow or another will drop by one week
end for a Gung Fu session.
Thanks again for everything and
do not forget to send me the
list.

Bruce

Dear George,

Your work, everyone of them, is fantastic. Not only are they professional, they are simply artistic. As usual, everyone here has high praise for your art. I, myself, do appreciate very much for your taking time off to do all those wonderful things for me. Thanks a lot George.

I'm sorry to say that I've lost your list for autograph. So will you please send me another one. Tell Dave Young of the delay too.

Upon my arrival, my agent called to let me know of CBS, proposal for a one hr. serial — kind of like I spy called "Hawaii 5-0." Looks good. will let you know what develops.

Will probably start tour next month but somehow or another will drop by one weekend for a Gung Fu session.

Thanks again for everything and do not forget to send me the list.

Bruce

Bruce, Brandon and Linda at a party.

I always liked the letters I got from Bruce that discussed the equipment I had made for him. I am truly happy that I could be part of his life in such an important way. We shared countless hours developing this equipment so he could improve his method of exercise, which set the path to his physical greatness. I also made many signs for Bruce. They were like little affirmations he would hang on the wall or put on his desk. Those were great times.

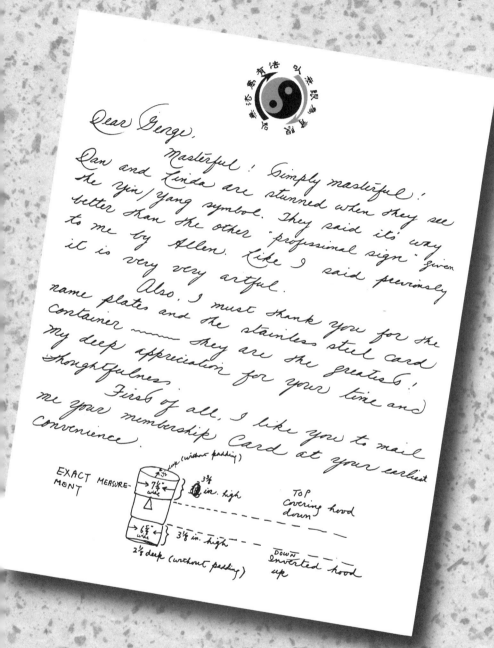

Dear George,

Masterful! Simply masterful! Dan and Linda are stunned when they see the Yin/Yang symbol. They said it's way better than the other "professional sign" given to me by Allen. Like I said previously it is very very artful.

Also, I must thank you for the name plates and the stainless steel card container ——— they are the greatest! My deep appreciation for your time and thoughtfulness.

First of all, I like you to mail me your membership card at your earliest convenience.

EXACT MEASURE-
MENT

7½" wide
3¼" up (without padding)
3¾ in. high
6¾" wide
3⅛ in. high
2⅛ deep (without padding)

TOP
Covering hood
down

DOWN
Inverted hood
up

15

The drawing on the bottom 1st page gives the exact measurement. In comparison to a human head, the width 7¼" is from ear to ear, the height 3⅜" is from forehead to top of nose, and the deepness of 1½" is from front of head to back of head. Now to the bottom part, the neck, as on a human. The height 3⅛" is from underchin to bottom of neck above collar bone, the width 6⅝" is from the end of neck to the other, and the deepness of 2⅛ deep is from throat to the back of neck.

All the above measurement is made without padding. In other word, the exact measurement on the 標準 equipment. Another thing I like to point out is the fact that for the top the hood is covering over the head; however, for the bottom, the hood has to covered the neck inverted. In other word, bottom up.

Thank you once more for everything
Thank you ever so much

Bruce

While his brother Robert looks on, Bruce gets some air in Los Angeles during the late 1960s.

Dear George,

Masterful! Simply masterful! Dan and Linda are stunned when they see the Yin/Yang symbol. They said it's way better than the other "professional sign" given to me by Allen. Like I said previously it is very very artful.

Also, I must thank you for the name plates and the stainless steel card container — they are the greatest! My deep appreciation for your time and thoughtfulness.

First of all, I like you to mail me your membership card at your earliest convenience.

The drawing on the bottom 1st. page gives the exact measurements. In comparison to a human head, the width 7 1/4" is from ear to ear, the height 3 3/8" is from forehead to top of nose, and the deepness of 1 1/2" is from front of head to back of head. Now to the bottom part, the neck, as on a human. The height 3 1/8" is from under chin to bottom of neck above collar bone, the width 6 5/8" is from the end of the neck to the other, and the deepness of 2 1/8" deep is from throat to the back of neck. All the above measurement is made without padding. In other word, the exact measurement on the Bill Jee equipment. Another thing I like to point out is the fact that for the top, the hood is covering over the head; however, for the bottom, the hood has to cover the neck inverted, in other word, bottom up.

Thank you once more for everything.

Thank you ever so much

Bruce

A wooden yin/yang built for Bruce, who placed it in front of his desk.

*T*his letter brings back great memories for me. I remember going to see Bruce on the set of "The Green Hornet." At one point, Bruce made us part of the crew, and we participated in the shooting of a scene. So there we were: James Lee, Allen Joe and me. To give the impression Bruce was driving down a street, the three of us bounced up and down on his car bumper while he pretended to be driving. Later, Bruce took us over to see how "Batman" was shot. It was so funny to see Batman and Robin swinging from wires attached to the studio ceiling. When we were done there, we went to see how "Payton Place" was filmed. That was truly a wonderful day in my life.

Dear George,

Just a letter to see how my   March 31 1966
favorite student is coming along —— I'm
sorry that I couldn't teach you as we
planned because there is a slight change
in the 20ᵗʰ Century Fox deal. Probably James
Lee has told you about it; at any rate.
the "Green Hornet" is going to be on the air
this coming September. At present I'm taking
acting lesson from a very well known Jeff
Cory, the best drama coach here in Hollywood

I'll be giving private lesson
before the Serie starts. The prospective
students are so far Steve McQueen, Paul
Newman, James Gardner, Don Gordon, and
Vic Damone. The fee will be around
$25 an hour.

Understand you are going to start
with James again. It's nice and you
should stick with it and go as often
as you can. James is really not a good

teacher, and you know what I'm talking about. However, as for now, you can gain some knowledge from him. Keep asking questions and follow what I've told you that nite.

I'm developing fully and fully the 5 way of attacking and even James doesn't know it. Next time when I see you I hope I'll have time to show you and teach you because George you've got what it takes and your attitude certainly deserves the best.

The "Green Hornet" will start shooting the end of May and I'll be busy like hell but the first chance I have I like to take a trip to Oakland and we should go out dinner.

Take care my friend and drop me a line when you have time. By the way, unless you know him well, do not give my address to the students. Thanks.

Bruce

George and Bruce on the set of "The Green Hornet."

Dear George,

Just a letter to see how my favorite student is coming along — I'm sorry that I couldn't teach you as we planned because there is a slight change in the 20th Century Fox deal. Probably James Lee has told you about it; at any rate, the *"Green Hornet"* is going to be on the air this coming September. At present I'm taking acting lessons from a very well known Jeff Cory, the best drama coach here in Hollywood.

I'll be giving private lessons before the series starts. The prospective students are so far Steve McQueen, Paul Newman, James Gardner, Dan Gordan and Vic Damone. The fee will be around $25 an hour.

Understand you are going to start with James again. It's nice and you should stick with it and go as often as you can. James is really not a good teacher, and you know what I'm talking about. However, as for now, you can gain some knowledge from him. Keep asking questions and follow what I've told you that nite.

I'm developing fully and fully the 5 Way of Attacking and even James doesn't know it. Next time when I see you I hope I'll have time to show you and teach you because George you've got what it takes and your attitude certainly deserves the best.

The *"Green Hornet"* will start shooting the end of May and I'll be busy like hell but the first chance I have I like to take a trip to Oakland and we should go out to dinner.

Take care my friend and drop me a line when you have time. By the way, unless you know him well, do not give my address to the students. Thanks.

Bruce.

When I read this letter, it takes me back to the times I used to make Bruce different kinds of punching bags. They came in all sizes. Bruce truly liked the craftsmanship on the bags. They were durable, and he liked that.

Dear George,

    Thank you very much for those two punching bags.

    Ian picked me up this morning and he will put one of the bag up on the wall in the gym to-day.

    Well, to-morrow I'll take off again and it will be a long trip - - - - - - -

    Again thank you for those bags, and as usual they are terrific

Bruce

See you this week-end

6 Transcription

Dear George,

Thank you very much for those two punching bags!

Dan picked me up this morning and he will put one of the bag up on the wall in the gym to-day.

Well, to-morrow I'll take off again and it will be a long trip —

Again thank you for those bags, and as usual they are terrific.

Bruce

See you this week-end

Bruce at a party.

*T*his letter really takes me back. I remember Bruce doing a demonstration on stage with James Lee. Bruce executed a technique, but James moved forward way too much. As a result, Bruce hit him with full force, making his nose bleed heavily. When it happened, the audience became dead silent and just stared at the two men on stage. The accident occurred because James was off balance. James stumbled toward Bruce's punch and was hit. It was serious at that time, but now it is quite humorous. In this letter, Bruce also mentioned a pair of shoes I made for him. He wanted a pair of shoes with a metal lining in between the sole and bottom of the shoe. This was really a hard job for me, but I finally was able to make them the way he liked it. I asked Bruce what these shoes were for, and he told me the shoes were to kick people in the shins if they got too close. When he left the set of "The Green Hornet," people would grab him and ask for an autograph. He said someone once tore his shirt off and hurt him. Bruce was truly a funny guy. It just shows you that he was constantly coming up with great ideas that revolved around his martial arts skill.

Dear George, I'm glad you made it
to the luau. Allen Joe went too but
he couldn't get in. Anyway, I'm
glad it's over as I'm sick of
demonstration.

The two punching pad is
out of sight and Dan flipped when
he saw them. He said it's too beauty
to be used in class. We might as well
know that whatever you make you
turn is into a masterpiece. Terrific.

There will be a birthday, too,
together party at my house on Nov 25,
Sat. So let me know if you can make
it for this week-end and come up
on Friday nite (NOV. 24). I'll send you
a round trip ticket. So do let
me know as soon as you can. Do not
tell James or anyone I'm sending
you the ticket though.

Again, thank you for your
"cool" equipment.

Bruce

P.S. The shoes are really nicely
put together

31

Dear George,

I'm glad you made it to the luau. Allen Joe went too but he couldn't get in. Anyway, I'm glad it's over as I'm sick of demonstrations.

The two punching pad is out of sight and Dan flipped when he saw them. He said it's too beautiful to be used in class. We might as well know that whatever you make you turn it into a masterpiece. Terrific.

There will be a birthday get together party at my house on Nov. 25, Sat. So let me know if you can make it for this week-end and come up on Friday nite (Nov. 24). I'll send you a round trip ticket. So do let me know as soon as you can. Do not tell James or anyone I'm sending you the ticket though.

Again thank you for your "cool" equipment

Bruce

P.S. The shoes are really nicely put together.

From left to right: George Lee, Bruce Lee, James Lee and Allen Joe on the set of "The Green Hornet."

ruce's love for the grip machine that I made for him is what stands out in my mind about this letter. His forearms were incredible, and he always praised me for my work on this piece of equipment. To this day, when I see Bruce posing in a magazine or on film, his forearms always jump out at me.

Dear George,

It was nice of you to call.

June 25 1966

I'll probably come down one weekend in the middle of next month to pick up some of the weights. By the way, the grip machine you made for me is darn good, and it helps me in my training very much. If and when I make the trip, I will let you know, as I like to get together with you.

Thanks again for your thoughtful call, and do drop me a line when you have the time.

Take care my friend

June 25 1966

Dear George,

It was nice of you to call.

I'll probably come down one weekend in the middle of next month to pick up some of the weights. By the way, the grip machine you made for me is darn good, and it helps me in my training very much. If and when I make the trip, I will let you know, as I like to get together with you.

Thanks again for your thoughtful call, and do drop me a line when you have the time.

Take care my friend

Bruce

James Lee and his children visit Bruce on the set of "The Green Hornet."

*O*nce again, this is a letter in which Bruce mentioned the bags I made for him. Bruce used to hang the bags, which were all different sizes, everywhere. I remember a bag I made for him that was very small. We were at dinner one night when he took out this bag and put it on the table. He then started doing finger jabs on it. Bruce was constantly training. He was one of a kind.

George, the master maker,

Thanks for those four "magnificent" throwing bags! Man, they are cool — really cool.

With appreciation

Bruce

9 Transcription

George, the master maker,

Thanks for those four "magnificent" throwing bags! Man, they are cool — really Cool.

With appreciation

Bruce

George poses with the stars of "The Green Hornet," Van Williams and Bruce Lee.

I remember making many different types of kicking and punching shields for Bruce. I used to enjoy making them. Bruce also mentioned in this letter that he and James Coburn were working on a project that was supposed to be called "The Silent Flute." Bruce was truly excited about doing this, and he looked forward to working with Coburn. I can remember Bruce telling me one of the parts he was going to play was a wise blind man. Bruce actually had contact lenses made up for the role. He was very close to doing that project, and it would have been a great one.

George,

After experimenting on the shield, we find that because of the thickness and extra weight, it absorbs the shock much better. Therefore the holder is not as miserable as before. Thanks to you.

As I mentioned, we are preparing a script, Coburn, Silliphant – and I. Coburn and I will star in it. We hope to start shooting the end of the year, if Coburn's schedule is opened. If not, then it has to be next March. At any rate, this will be the start of something really really big for me.

Take care my friend and
thank you once more

Bruce

George,

After experimenting on the shield, we find that because of the thickness and extra weight, it absorbs the shock much better. Therefore the holder is not as miserable as before, thanks to you.

As I mentioned, we are preparing a script, Coburn, Silliphant and I. Coburn and I will star in it. We hope to start shooting the end of the year, if Coburn's schedule is opened. If not, then it has to be next March. At any rate, this will be the start of something really really big for me.

Take care my friend and thank you once more

Bruce

George, Bruce, Allen and James on the set of "The Green Hornet."

I liked James Coburn as an actor, and I asked Bruce to get me an autographed picture from him. Bruce eventually sent me a signed photo from James, and it was great to get something like that from such a big movie star.

George,

A letter to let you know that Coburn's picture should be on its way next week. I just returned from the East Coast with him. McQueen is in Europe, so his has to wait. Just want to let you know I haven't forgotten my friend.

My mother and brother are here. They are presently staying with me.

Things are going great with me — will let you know when they develop.

Take Care —

Bruce

George,

A letter to let you know that Coburn's picture should be on its way next week. I just returned from the East Coast with him. Mc Queen is in Europe, so his has to wait. Just want to let you know I haven't forgotten my friend.

My mother and brother are here. They are presently staying with me.

Things are going great with me — will let you know when they develop.

Take care   Bruce

Dear George,

Sorry for the delay, but thank you for the punching bag you have made for me. It will help my punching.

Thank you

Sincerely,

James Coburn

To George,
Thank you +
Best Wishes.

James Coburn

*T*his letter is just another example of the appreciation Bruce showed to me for making equipment for him.

George,

Finally moved but still unpacking and a lot of rearranging. It's a heck of a job but I must take time out to once more thank you for that magnificent job you did on that finger jab equipment. I've already heard from James that the base for the leg stretcher will be terrific. Actually I need not have him to inform me on that, Man, like everything you touch has to be beautiful or else you won't deliver it.

I'm flying up this week-end, give me a call at James and we'll get together. I will sharpen at least one of your technique with my newly found training method. Okay, George.

Take Care my friend

Bruce

George,

Finally moved but still unpacking and a lot of rearranging. It's a hell of a job but I must take time out to once more thank you for that magnificent job you did on that finger jab equipment. I've already heard from James that the base for the leg stretcher will be terrific. Actually I need not have him to inform me on that. Man, like everything you touch has to be beautiful or else you won't deliver it.

I'm flying up this week-end, give me a call at James and we'll get together. I will sharpen at least one of your technique with my newly found training method. Okay, George.

Take Care my friend

Bruce

Bruce Lee, Dan Inosanto (center) and Allen Joe having lunch, circa 1960s.

*I*n this letter from Bruce, he expressed how he liked the kicking and punching equipment I made for him. Bruce was always asking me to make more of this type of equipment because he beat up the boards pretty good. Therefore, he always needed me to make more for him. Furthermore, his friends also wanted boards. Bruce also mentioned a film project that he was working on with Steve McQueen. I never heard what happened to this project, but I know Bruce was excited about it.

Bruce, alongside James Lee, who is holding one of George Lee's creations.

George,

Remember the kicking and punching padded boards you made for me well, after using them for a while, I have come to many improvements. When you have time, can you make an extra kicking board and punching board for me? Your kicking board is top for kicking, no heavy bag can replace it. The accompany sheets will describe the added improvement.

Steve McQueen, after he completes his movie in Frisco, will get a writer and start on a Gung Fu movie with him and I in it. So this is a start-toward the movie.

On April 6 I probably will come up because there is a so called "National Gung Fu Exhibition" held in Frisco — a bunch of guys will be in there, including Chris Chen, the president by the way, and the runner 李小龍 will show up to scare hell out of them.

Take Care

How do you like new cards — am teaching a few guys private lessons now.

George,

Remember the kicking and punching padded boards you made for me — well, after using them for a while, I have come to many improvements. When you have the time, can you make an extra kicking board and punching board for me? Your kicking board is top for kicking, no heavy bag can replace it. The accompany sheets will describe the added improvements.

Steve McQueen, after he completes his movie in frisco, will get a writer and start on a Gung Fu movie with him and I in it. So this is a start toward the movie.

On April 6 I probably will come up because there is a so called "National Gung Fu Exhibition," held in Frisco — a bunch of guys will be in there, including Chris Chan, the president by the way, and the runner Wong Jack Man. I will show up to scare hell out of them.

Take Care

Bruce

How do you like new cards — am teaching a few guys private lessons now.

James and Bruce posing for the camera, circa 1960s.

*T*his is another letter in which Bruce talked about some of the things I made for him. It made me feel good when Bruce told me how he and others appreciated what I created.

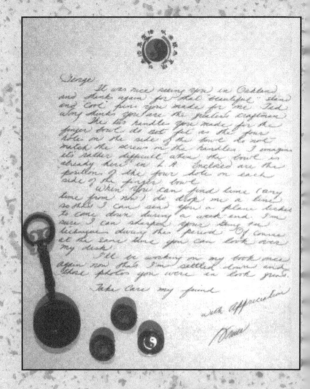

George,

It was nice seeing you in Oakland and thanks again for that "beautiful" shined and "cool" pins you made for me. Ted Wong thinks you are the greatest craftsman.

The two handles you made for the finger bowl do not fit as the four holes on the side of the bowl do not match the screws on the handles. I imagine it's rather difficult — when the bowl is already here in L.A. Enclosed are the positions of the four hole on each side of the finger bowl.

When you can find time (any time from now) do drop me a line so that I can send you a plane ticket to come down during a week-end. I'm sure I can sharpen your Gung Fu technique during this period. Of course at the same time you can look over my desk.

I'll be working on my book once again now that I'm settled down and those photos you were in look great.

Take care my friend

with Appreciation

Bruce

George,

It was nice seeing you in Oakland and thanks again for that "beautiful" stained and "cool" pins you made for me. Ted Wong thinks you are the greatest craftman.

The two handles you made for the finger bowl do not fit as the four holes on the side of the bowl do not match the screws on the handles. I imagine it's rather difficult when the bowl is already here in L.A. Enclosed are the positions of the four holes on each side of the finger bowl.

When you can find the time (any time from now) do drop me a line so that I can send you a plane ticket to come down during a week-end. I'm sure I can sharpen your Gung Fu techniques during this period. Of course at the same time you can look over my desk.

I'll be working on my book once again now that I'm settled down and those photos you were in look great.

Take care my friend

With Appreciation

Bruce

The four musketeers: George Lee, Allen Joe, Bruce Lee and James Lee.

This is a letter from Bruce in which he informed me that he was coming to Oakland and wanted to get together so we could train. My training sessions with Bruce incorporated physical training and philosophy. Those times were truly great.

George,

I am coming to Oakland on May 26, this coming Friday at around 5 P.M. and will go to James' Fremont class for a short lecture-type lesson for his students. Then I would like to get together with you, James and Allen for a Gung Fu session (probably next day, Sat.) However, if you can go to the Fremont class with us you can come and leave your car at James'. I think you do know some of the students there.

At any rate, hope to see you this trip, and that nothing sudden comes up to prevent me from coming.

Take Care.

Bruce

George

I am coming to Oakland on May 26, this coming Friday at around 5 P.M. and will go to James Fremont class for a short lecture-type lesson for his students. Then I would like to get together with you, James and Allen for a Gung Fu session (probably next day, Sat.) However, if you can go to the Fremont class with us you can come and leave your car at James. I think you do know some of the students there.

At any rate, hope to see you this trip, and that nothing sudden comes up to prevent me from coming.

Take Care

Bruce

Bruce and George having dinner.

Regards From A Friend

Here is a letter that showed Bruce's concern for my well-being. Bruce was a giving friend and he truly cared about others.

George,

I heard from James that you didn't feel good. I hope you're much better by now.

Take Care my friend

Bruce

George,

I heard from James that you didn't feel good. I hope you're much better by now.

Take Care my friend

Bruce

Despite his busy schedule, Bruce consistently found time to keep in touch with George Lee.

I remember when Bruce and I would go out to eat and discuss the martial arts and philosophy. Those times were great.

Genge,

Will be coming up to Oakland
this coming Friday (Feb. 16).
See you then

Bruce

17 Transcription

George,

   Will be coming up to Oakland this coming Friday (Feb. 16).

   See you then

                              Bruce

Bruce, Linda and Brandon celebrating a birthday.

*T*his is another letter about equipment and different events that surrounded Bruce's life.

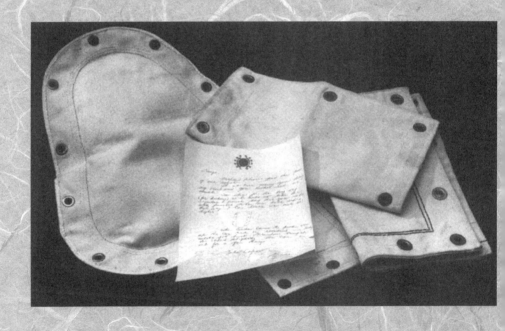

George,

Enclosed please find the pins of our school.

It was nice seeing you during my visit and you looked well as usual. One idea for the long bag (for kicking) is to make it like the regular punch bag that you made with punched holes on both sides. That way I can lower or make it higher.

When Linda came to pick me up the car had an accident — lucky nobody got hurt. Brandon bumped his head slightly. The car is out for a few days.

Take Care

Bruce

George,

Enclosed please find the pins of our school.

It was nice seeing you during my visit and you looked well as usual.

One idea for the long bag (for kicking) is to make it like the regular punch bag that you made with punched holes on both sides. That way I can lower or make it higher

When Linda came to pick me up the car had an accident — lucky nobody got hurt. Brandon bumped his head slightly. The car is out for a few day

Take care   Bruce

Bruce in action on the set of "The Green Hornet."

*T*his letter means a lot to me because Bruce told me that he considered me a close friend. I never heard Bruce say this to many others, so I took it to heart. This letter made me feel pretty good.

George,

I tried like hell, but I just can't get away during the Thanksgiving week-end. I would very much like to come because you're one of my very close friend. I want you to know that.

As soon as I have things clear here — ("I've been very busy working") — I would come up and give you a call.

By the way, James Coburn ("Our man flint") would like to have one of your wall bag. Can you get him one?

Will talk to you soon.

Thank you again for your kind invitation.

Bruce

George,

I tried like hell, but I just can't get away during the Thanksgiving week-end. I would very much like to come because you're one of my very close friends. I want you to know that.

As soon as I have things clear here — (I've been very busy working) — I would come up and give you a call.

By the way, James Coburn (*"Our Man Flint"*) would like to have one of your wall bags. Can you get him one?

Will talk to you soon

Thank you again for your kind invitation

Bruce

Bruce looking sharp for the camera.

*W*hat stands out most of all in this letter is Bruce's reference to his workout program. As you can see, Bruce truly worked hard on getting himself into great shape. Many people look at Bruce in magazines or movies and do not realize the work he put in to get into that great shape. Not only was Bruce a well-rounded martial artist, he also lifted weights.

George,

Haven't written for a little while. How are things?

Your wall punching bags have definitely helped in my daily training. I've started the training on Christmas Eve, my 1968 resolution. I now train an average of 2½ hrs. a day, including hand exercises, leg exercise, running, isometric, stomach exercise, sparring exercise, free hand exercise. Your training equipments all help in my program.)

Thanks.

Allen Joe must have told you about James Lee's surprise party on Jan 26 (Friday nite) — I'll fly in that nite without letting him know. Do your best to be there; after all, you are one of the very important member. So take care my friend, and my best to your wife and family.

Bruce

By the way, could you give me your home phone number once more —

George

Haven't written for a little while, how are things?

Your wall punching bags have definitely helped in my daily training. I've started the training on Christmas eve. My 1968 resolution. I now train an average of $2\frac{1}{2}$ hrs. a day, including hand exercises, leg exercises, running, isometric, stomach exercises, sparring exercises, free hand exercises. Your training equipments all help in my program. Thanks.

Allen Joe must have told you about James Lee's surprise party on Jan 26 (Friday nite) — I'll fly in that nite without letting him know. Do your best to be there; after all, you are one of the very important members.

So take care my friend, and my best to your wife and family.

Bruce

By the way, could you give me your home phone number once more —

Bruce taking the time out for a photo at the Jhoon Rhee Karate Championships.

*B*ruce kept in touch to let me know about projects he had in the works. Bruce used to travel a lot, and he did many shows and exhibitions. I remember he was always working on something.

George, I still feel bad about that mixed up date. I thought it was Sept 29 (Sunday).

I'll be leaving for Mississippi with Steve. The project on Jeet Kune Do as a movie is taking another step. Stirling Silliphant (In the Heat of the Nite) is involved to write the script. We will be getting together and roll. After that I'll be flying to New York for a few days. Of course I'm moving too. As of next Monday, my address will be

2551 Roscomare Rd.
Los Angeles, Calif. 90024.

It's a pretty "Cool" house located inside Bel-air. As soon as I have the phone in, I'll let you know.

Anyway, let me know if you can come down in Nov. 27. Maybe we should arrange it at a different date. At any rate, the next day will be Thanks giving.

Take Care my friend.

Bruce

87

George,

I still feel bad about that mixed up date. I thought it was Sept 29 (Sunday).

I'll be leaving for Mississippi with Steve. The project on Jeet Kune Do as a movie is taking another step. Stirling Silliphant (*In The Heat of The Nite*) is involved to write the script. We will be getting together and roll. After that I'll be flying to New York for a few days.

Of course in the midst of all these I'm moving too. As of next Monday, my address will be

2551 Roscomare Rd.
Los Angeles, Calif. 90024.

It's a pretty "cool" house located inside Bel Air. As soon as I have the phone in, I'll let you know.

Anyway, let me know if you can come down in Nov. 27. Maybe we should arrange it at a different date. At any rate, the next day will be Thanks giving.

Take care my friend

Bruce

Sporting glasses, Bruce shows a different look.

*I*n this letter, Bruce praised me for
making more equipment for him.
He also drew a diagram of headgear
that he wanted me to make. Bruce was
a great artist, and he loved to draw.

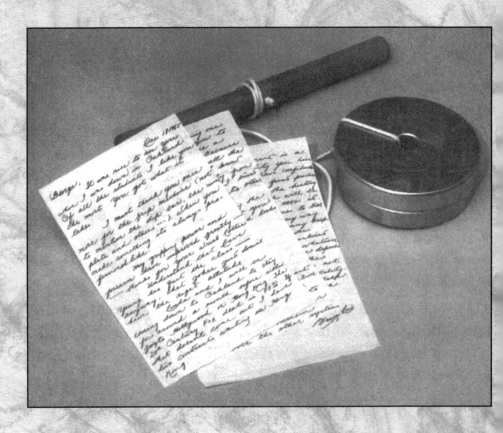

George,   Dec. 18 1965

It was nice to see you when I was down in Oakland. Of all the students I like you the most. You got what it takes.

I must thank you once more for the grip machine (not to mention the dip bar, the name plate and others---). When you make something it's always pro-fessional like.

My gripping power and forearm have improved greatly— thanks for your wrist roller. Understand that Dave Young has quit the class— anyway, that guy just doesn't have the right attitude.

Linda and I will be coming down to Oakland to stay for around a month before either going to Hollywood or Hong Kong. The 20th Century Fox deal is 852. If that doesn't come out I have two contracts waiting in Hong Kong.

During this coming one month stay I want you to drop by at least once a week at the house. Because I want to show you all the Gung Fu techniques. I know you will benefit greatly from these instructions and I trust you will not show it to other students.

I'm ~~one's~~ drawing the following diagrams to show you how a naval head-guard looks like.

FRONT VIEW

SIDE VIEW

The protective equipment is the most important invention in Gung Fu. It WILL raise the standard of Gung Fu to unbelievable height. In order for Gung Fu to remain supreme over the other systems the protective equipment is a must. With the ability you have in making things, I have confidence in your building the first practical protective equipment in the history of Gung Fu. Your work will be remembered. Gung Fu NEEDS it.

I've written James to tell him to help you in every way he can. If you need any help call him. Start with this great plan at your earliest convenience and devote whatever time you have. This plan depends on YOU because knowing the rest of the guys, they do not have the incentive or the ability. James should be able to help you some IF he isn't busy.

Take care of yourself
my friend
Bruce Lee

Dec. 18 1965

George,

It was nice to see you when I was down in Oakland. Of all the students I like you the most. You got what it takes.

I must thank you once more for the grip machine (not to mention the dip bar, the name plate and others —). When you make something it's always professional like.

My gripping power and forearm have improved greatly — thanks for your wrist Roller.

Understand that Dave Young has quit the class — anyway, that guy just doesn't have the right attitude.

Linda and I will be coming down to Oakland to stay for around a month before either going to Hollywood or Hong Kong. The 20th Century Fox deal is 85%. If that doesn't come out I have two contracts waiting in Hong Kong.

During this coming one month stay I want you to drop by at least once a week at the house. Because I want to show you all the Gung Fu techniques. I know you will benefit greatly from these instructions and I trust you will not show it to other students.

I'm drawing the following diagrams to show you how a naval head-guard looks like.

Side View

Front view

The protective equipment is the most important invention in Gung Fu. It WILL raise the standard of Gung Fu to unbelievable height. In order for Gung Fu to remain supreme over the other systems the protective equipment is a must. With the ability you have in making things, I have confidence in your building the first practical protective equipment in the history of Gung Fu. Your work will be remembered. Gung Fu NEEDS it.

I've written James to tell him to help you in every way he can. If you need any help call him. Start with this great plan at your earliest convenience and devote whatever time you have. This plan depends on YOU because knowing the rest of the guys, they do not have the incentive or the ability. James should be able to help you some if he isn't busy.

Take care of yourself my friend

Bruce Lee

*T*his letter brings back some great memories. Among other things, Bruce talked about filming "Batman." Of course, we all know by now that Bruce did the "Green Hornet." One of the shows featured the "Green Hornet meets Batman and Robin." Bruce had many stories to tell about this. I will just say this. Bruce was the better fighter. Next, Bruce drew some diagrams that he wanted me to make into signs. These signs, which show the path one takes in Bruce's system, became famous after his passing. Bruce felt that these illustrations were very important to show people the philosophy behind the art. There is also a diagram of a tombstone, which illustrates how one can be swallowed up by the classical mess of the so-called many kung-fu styles. This also became famous after Bruce's passing.

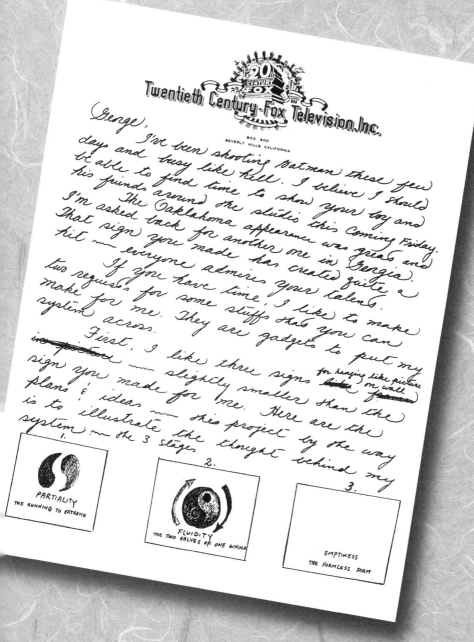

Twentieth Century-Fox Television, Inc.

BOX 900
BEVERLY HILLS, CALIFORNIA

George,

I've been shooting Batman these few days and busy like hell. I believe I should be able to find time to show your toy and his friends around the studio this coming Friday.

The Oaklahoma appearance was great and I'm asked back for another one in Georgia. That sign you made has created quite a hit — everyone admires your talent.

If you have time, I like to make two requests for some stuffs that you can make for me. They are gadgets to put my system across.

First, I like three signs for hanging like picture on wall — slightly smaller than the sign you made for me. Here are the plans & ideas — this project by the way is to illustrate the thought behind my system — the 3 stages

1.
PARTIALITY
THE RUNNING TO EXTREME

2.
FLUIDITY
THE TWO HALVES OF ONE WHOLE

3.
EMPTINESS
THE FORMLESS FORM

<u>Explanation for the three signs</u> (same black shining background as the sign you made)

FIRST SIGN

Here all we need is one red half and one gold half of the Yin Yang symbol. HOWEVER <u>no</u> dot is need on either halves; in other word it is just plain red with no gold dot, or just plain gold with no red dot (this serves to illustrate extreme softness (like 太極) or /and extreme hardness (like 沾家). So just follow the drawing and also put the phrase — PARTIALITY — THE RUNNING TO EXTREME on the black board

SECOND SIGN

Exact Yin Yang symbol like the sign you made for me except there is <u>no</u> Chinese characters around the symbol. Of course, the phrase — FLUIDITY — THE TWO HALVES OF ONE WHOLE will be on the black board.

THIRD SIGN

Just a shinny black board with nothing on it except the phrase EMPTINESS — THE FORMLESS FORM.

The three signs have to be the same size because they illustrate the three stages of cultivation. Please do make them like the sign you made for me aluminum symbol and shinny back board

The second gadget I have in mind is used to dramatize the not too alive way of the classical so called Kung Fu styles. What I have in mind is a miniature "tomb stone" and here is the drawing

IN MEMORY
OF
A ONCE FLUID MAN
CRAMMED AND DISTORTED
BY
THE CLASSICAL MESS

I'm sure you know how a grave looks like and make it with any material you like (aluminium tomb stone is fine) and at any size you want. Not too small though, because it's for display.

Call me collect if you have any problem

Thank you in antisipation   Bruce

23 Transcription

George,

   I've been shooting Batman these few days and busy like hell. I believe I should be able to find time to show your boy and his friends around the studio this coming Friday.

   The Oklahoma appearance was great and I'm asked back for another one in Georgia. That sign you made has created quite a hit — everyone admires your talents.

   If you have time, I like to make two requests for some stuffs that you can make for me. They are gadgets to put my system across.

   First, I like three signs for hanging like pictures on wall — slightly smaller than the sign you made for me. Here are the plans & ideas — this project by the way is to illustrate the thought behind my system — the 3 stages

   Explanation for the three signs (same black shining background as the sign you made)

   FIRST SIGN

here all we need is one red half and one gold half of the yin yang symbol. HOWEVER no dot is need on either halves; in other word it is just plain red with no gold dot, or just plain gold with no red dot (this serves to illustrate extreme softness (like Tygik) or/and extreme hardness (like Hung Sar). So just follow the drawing and also put the phrase — PARTIALITY — THE RUNNING TO EXTREME on the black board.

SECOND SIGN

Exact yin yang symbol like the sign you made for me except there is no Chinese characters around the symbol. Of course, the phrase — FLUIDITY — THE TWO HALVES OF ONE WHOLE will be on the black board.

THIRD SIGN

Just a shinny black board with nothing on it except the phrase EMPTINESS — THE FORMLESS FORM.

The three signs have to be the same size because they illustrate the three stages of cultivation. Please

23 Transcription

do make them like the sign you made for me aluminum symbol and shinny black boards.

The second gadget I have in mind is used to dramatize the not too alive Way of the classical so called Kung Fu styles. What I have in mind is a miniature "tomb stone" and here is the drawing

I'm sure you know how a grave looks like and make it with any material you like (aluminum tomb stone is fine) and at any size you want. NOT too small though, because it's for display.

Call me collect if you have any problem.

Thank you in anticipation,

Bruce

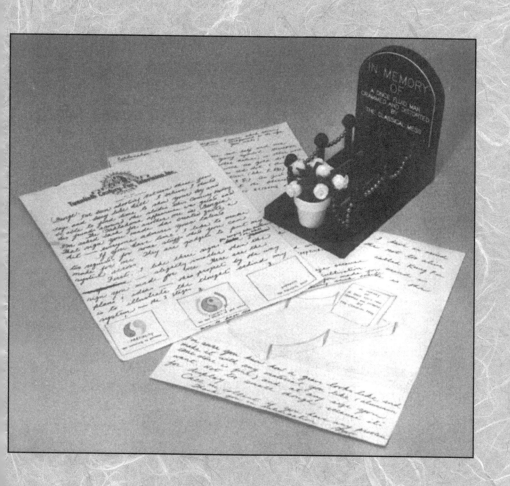

*I*n this letter, Bruce thanked me for sending padding for a shield. Bruce always shared his gratitude with me and treated me like a big brother.

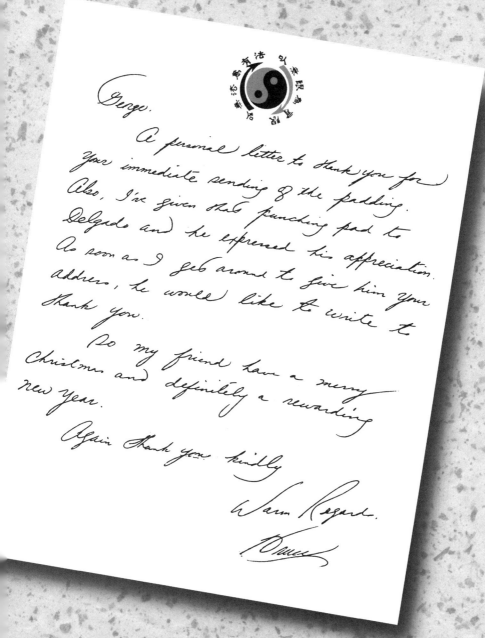

George,

A personal letter to thank you for your immediate sending of the padding. Also, I've given that punching pad to Delgado and he expressed his appreciation. As soon as I get around to give him your address, he would like to write to thank you.

So my friend have a merry Christmas and definitely a rewarding new year.

Again thank you kindly

Warm Regards,

Dan

George

A personal letter to thank you for your immediate sending of the padding. Also, I've given that punching pad to Delgado and he expressed his appreciation. As soon as I get around to give him your address, he would like to write to thank you.

So my friend have a Merry Christmas and definitely a rewarding New Year.

Again thank you kindly

Warm Regards.

Bruce

Bruce and an actress behind the scenes in one of his last films before he left for the mainland.

*T*his letter reminds me that Bruce was not the only one who used the equipment that I made for him. Many others liked it, too, and many times Bruce would have me make equipment for other people, like Danny Inosanto. Even though I did not live in Los Angeles at that time, I feel we were all family sharing something special.

Dear George,

Too bad you aren't here. You should have heard comments from the fellows down here! "Is he a pro artist? I don't believe this!" (Dan said that) and many many more on the fine work you've created. As for me, they are terrific!! Thanks once more for the many hours you've put in; you're the greatest.

Bruce

25 Transcription

Dear George,

Too bad you aren't here. You should have heard comments from the fellows down here! "Is he a pro artist." "I don't believe this!" (Dan said that) and many many more on the fine work you've created. As for me, they are terrific!! Thanks once more for the many hours you've put in; you're the greatest.

Bruce

*I*n this letter, Bruce commented on some equipment I made for him. Bruce and I had a close friendship, and we shared many ideas, which made for many incredible memories.

George,

A masterpiece indeed!
my appreciation my friend
—— not only to the workmanship (that is always top!) but
particularly to your thoughtfulness.
Thank you George

Peace - Love - Brotherhood

Bruce

George,

A masterpiece indeed! My appreciation my friend — not only to the workmanship (that is always top!) but particularly to your thoughtfulness.

Thank you George

Peace – Love – Brotherhood

Bruce

George made this brass halperd for Bruce, but he was never able to give it to him.

*B*ruce touched base with me to let me know what he was doing. Letters like this bring back memories of the simple times he and I shared.

George,

I'm coming to Oakland this coming Monday nite around 9:30 P.M. I'll probably give you a call.

I'll stay till Thursday afternoon and then will take off to New York for an appearance at the All American Open Karate Championship. I'll stay there for four days then I'll go to Seattle for a few days and then will come back to Oakland for a couple of days before I'll take off to Springfield, Mass. for another appearance.

Plan on coming down for the photo-shooting on the week-end of July 8.

Will talk to you when I see you.

Bruce

George,

I'm coming to Oakland this coming Monday nite around 9:30 P.M. I'll probably give you a call.

I'll stay till Thursday afternoon and then will take off to New York for an appearance at the All American Open Karate Championship. I'll stay there for four days then I'll go to Seattle for a few days and then will come back to Oakland for a couple of days before I'll take off to Springfield, Mass. for another appearance.

Plan on coming down for the photo-shooting on the week-end of July 8.

Will talk to you when I see you.

Bruce

Bruce in the early 1970s.

Letters of Appreciation

*H*ere are two letters of appreciation I received. Both meant a lot to me. One is from Bruce's wife, Linda, and one is from Steve McQueen.

MRS. BRUCE LEE

Dear George,

March 22, 1969

Many thanks for remembering me on my birthday. You are always so thoughtful. We are in the final stages of preparation for our next-born now. As the time grows shorter I can think of so many things to do.

Bruce has enjoyed the equipment you have made for him and they are such a big aid in teaching. You are truly a master craftman.

If you plan to visit this way anytime, be sure to let us know. My regards to your wife.

Sincerely,

Linda

FROM STEVE McQUEEN

Thank you very much for the
green bean bag.

This scroll was presented to George in April 1999. It reads:

To George Lee

*   In appreciation for your dedication, timeless effort and unselfishness to help your dear friend, Bruce Lee, achieve his goal to preserve and perpetuate his art. The Bruce Lee Educational Foundation thanks you for your lifelong devotion and dedicated service.*

125

Regards From A Friend

Captured Moments

Painting by Steve Walling

Bruce behind the wheel.

Bruce with his sister Phoebe in a heartfelt moment.

128

Bruce in Hong Kong in one of his childhood films.

Regards From A Friend

Bruce and his brothers and sisters at a gathering in Hong Kong.

Bruce dancing with his girlfriend, Pearl Cho.

Bruce giving his younger brother Robert some cha cha instructions.

131

In Closing

In closing, I would like to reiterate that I was truly fortunate to have met Bruce Lee. Having read this book, I also hope that you've learned a great deal more about the "The Little Dragon."

These letters show Bruce Lee the man and Bruce Lee the legend, but most of all they show Bruce Lee my friend. Of course, Bruce had other close friends, and I'm sure they also have their own letters to share. I wanted to share mine because I feel that Bruce's image can be one-sided at times. It is important to recognize that Bruce Lee was a man who did great things, and we must not forget he worked very hard to accomplish those great things.

If Bruce Lee taught us anything at all, it would be that hard work and relentless dedication will open up many doors with endless possibilities. Bruce had goals, and he focused on those goals. And in the end, he accomplished those goals. Bruce was not superhuman; however, he was certainly a super human being.

Today, there are many people throughout the world who Bruce Lee has touched in many different ways. As a good friend of his, I can assure you that he would be proud to know that he has influenced so many individuals on the path to health and self-exploration.

There are great people like Dan Inosanto and Taky Kimura, both of whom Bruce appointed instructors. There were countless others like Ted Wong, who Bruce instructed. All of us have a piece of Bruce Lee in our memories and in our hearts.

Throughout the years, there have been disagreements on many levels regarding Bruce and how Bruce left his legacy. Let me just say that if we all take a step back and remember one moment that we shared with Bruce, and it makes us smile, then we all know we were part of his legacy. Let us remember that there are always two sides to a coin and that sometimes we do not have all the answers. I am just happy I can share moments in time with the many friends and fans of the late, great Bruce Lee.

— George Lee

Take Care my friend

Bruce Lee